THE
BLACKFEET
INDIANS

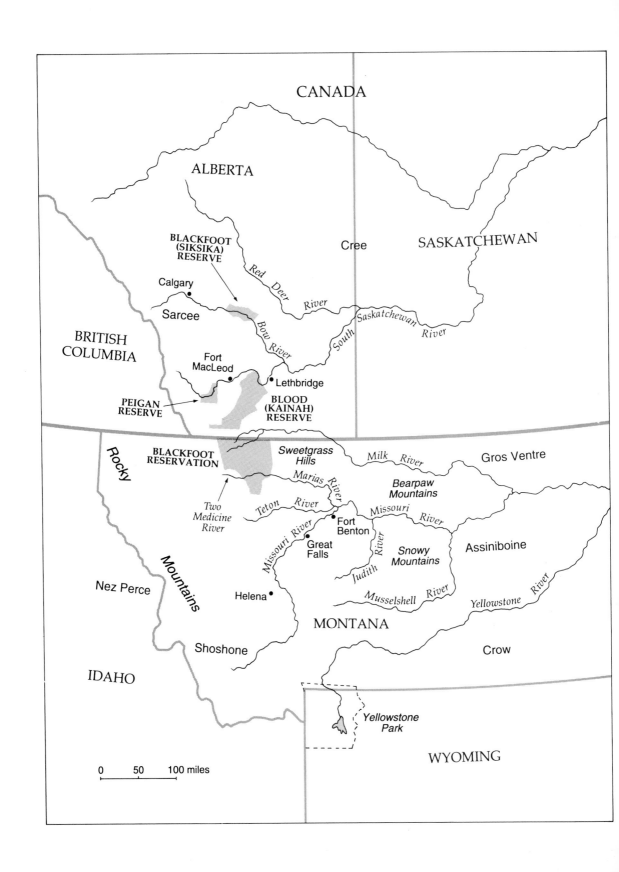

CANADA

ALBERTA

BLACKFOOT
(SIKSIKA)
RESERVE

Cree

SASKATCHEWAN

Calgary

Red Deer

River

South Saskatchewan River

Sarcee

BRITISH
COLUMBIA

Bow River

Fort
MacLeod

Lethbridge

PEIGAN
RESERVE

BLOOD
(KAINAH)
RESERVE

Rocky

BLACKFOOT
RESERVATION

*Sweetgrass
Hills*

Milk River

Gros Ventre

Marias River

*Bearpaw
Mountains*

Teton River

*Two
Medicine
River*

Missouri River

Missouri River

Fort
Benton

Great
Falls

Judith River

*Snowy
Mountains*

Assiniboine

Mountains

Nez Perce

Helena

Musselshell River

Yellowstone River

Shoshone

MONTANA

Crow

IDAHO

*Yellowstone
Park*

WYOMING

0   50   100 miles

THE JUNIOR LIBRARY OF
AMERICAN INDIANS

THE
BLACKFEET
INDIANS

Ann-Marie Hendrickson

CHELSEA JUNIORS 🌿

a division of CHELSEA HOUSE PUBLISHERS

FRONTISPIECE: Map showing present-day boundaries for the three Blackfeet reserves in Canada and the Blackfeet reservation in Montana.

CHAPTER TITLE ORNAMENT: Native American pictograph of a buffalo skull.

Chelsea House Publishers
EDITOR-IN-CHIEF Stephen Reginald
MANAGING EDITOR James D. Gallagher
PRODUCTION MANAGER Pamela Loos
ART DIRECTOR Sara Davis
PICTURE EDITOR Judy Hasday
SENIOR PRODUCTION EDITOR Lisa Chippendale

Staff for THE BLACKFEET INDIANS
ASSOCIATE EDITOR Kristine Brennan
DESIGN AND TYPOGRAPHY Duke & Company
PICTURE RESEARCHER Sandy Jones
COVER ILLUSTRATION Shelley Pritchett

3 5 7 9 8 6 4

Library of Congress Cataloging-in-Publication Data

Hendrickson, Ann-Marie.
The Blackfeet Indians / Ann-Marie Hendrickson.
    p. cm.
Includes bibliographical references and index.
Summary: Provides a history of these buffalo hunters of the northern plains from their acquisition of horses and forced assimilation by whites to their current life in Montana and Canada.
ISBN   0-7910-1659-5 (hc)
          0-7910-4466-1 (pbk)
1. Siksika Indians—History—Juvenile literature. [1. Siksika Indians. 2. Indians of North America.] I. Title.
E99.S54H46 1997
973'.04973—dc21   97-11888
                                                          CIP
                                                          AC

CONTENTS

*According to one version
of the Blackfeet creation
myth, Old Man fashioned
the prairies, the mountains,
and all living things out
of mud and clay.*

CHAPTER 1

A World of Abundance

To the Blackfeet Indians, Napi, or Old Man, was the master of all living things. He gave them life, food to eat, and land to call their own.

All of this didn't come about at once, though. Old Man worked very hard. Traveling from south to north, he made the Great Plains out of mud. He took care to give the landscape mountains and valleys so that the world would not look the same everywhere. To these he added tender shoots of grass, thick brush, and trees that bore sweet fruit. Old Man hid some treasures below the earth's surface, too: he planted wild turnips and carrots for the people and animals to eat.

But there were no people or animals until Old Man did his magic. After he finished making the land, he molded clay into human forms. He gave them life by blowing on them. Slowly, they started to take on the appearance of men and women. Old Man named these first people the *Siksika.* The people stood up and walked at his command. Some Blackfeet storytellers today say that Napi spent four days creating people.

Old Man's work was far from done, however. As soon as his people could walk and talk, they asked him for food. Old Man said nothing, but took more clay and molded it into buffalo shapes. At his beckoning the clay buffalo herd came to life and started running across the Plains. The buffalo were very large and powerful. "These are your food," he told the Siksika.

Old Man created animals of every shape and size by molding them out of clay and blowing upon them. Napi made birds to glide through the skies, gophers to dig holes in the ground, mice to scurry over it. He made strange animals, like paddle-tailed beavers and bad-smelling skunks, too. He also created bighorn sheep and pronghorn antelope. Old Man told the Siksika that it was all right for them to kill animals for meat or for furs—but that they must never waste any creature they hunted.

But Old Man still had some problems to solve. Some of the animals were not doing well where he had left them. The first bighorn sheep, with its heavy horns, could only lumber slowly across the prairie. Old Man wanted to help. Pulling the sheep by one of its horns, Old Man led it up to a high mountaintop and turned it loose. The bighorn sheep jumped fearlessly from cliff to cliff and seemed to like climbing ever higher. Old Man told the sheep to stay in the rocks and the mountains, for that was where it belonged.

While he was on the mountain, Old Man noticed that the first pronghorn antelope was also having trouble. Although it was strong like the bighorn sheep, the pronghorn ran so very fast that it fell off the high mountain peaks and got hurt. Old Man helped the pronghorn, too. He took it down to the prairie and let it go. When he saw how speedy the animal was on level ground, Old Man declared, "This is what you are suited for."

The people, like the animals, faced problems on the brand-new earth. Unlike the animals, they complained to Old Man. Although he had given the people buffalo and other animals to eat, he had not taught them how to hunt. Instead, the animals were hunting the people! The buffalo, with their huge bodies and sharp horns, were especially dangerous to the Siksika. Old Man promised to help.

True to his word, he went out into the woods and found a large stick and whittled it into a curved shape. Old Man then took some plant fibers and made string, which he tied to both ends of the curved stick. This was the first bow. To make an arrow, he caught a bird and plucked feathers from its wing. He tied these feathers to one end of a small stick, then tied a sharp stone to the opposite end.

Old Man taught the people how to use his invention. He promised them that once they mastered the bow and arrow, the Siksika would no longer need to run away from the buffalo. Old Man was right: the people were soon using their bows and arrows to hunt not only buffalo, but also many other kinds of creatures.

Now well-fed and warmly dressed, the Siksika never thought about death. Even Old Man forgot about it until, one day, he made a woman and a boy out of mud from a riverbank. As they stood by the river, he told them that he was Napi, the maker of all things. The woman then asked him how life worked. "Will there be no end to it?" she wondered.

Old Man had no answer ready, but he made

up a test to decide the people's fate. He picked up a buffalo chip (a dried piece of dung) and threw it into the river. "If it floats, people will die for four days and then come back to life. But if it sinks, death will be the end of them," he said. When the buffalo chip floated, the woman panicked. She didn't want to die—not even for four days. The woman hurled a stone into the water and said, "If this stone floats, then people will live forever. But if it sinks, then people will die forever."

Of course, the stone sank. "Perhaps it is better if people die forever," she reasoned. "That way, they will have sympathy for each other."

"You have chosen," Old Man agreed. "Let it be the law."

A few days later, the woman's son died. She pleaded with Old Man to change the law back to the one he had made, which said that people only died for four days. He refused, reminding the woman that it was her own choice that people should die.

Even though they no longer lived forever, the Siksika became numerous, spreading out over the land and forming the five tribes. These were the Siksika, Kainah, and Peigan (or Piegan) peoples (Blackfeet groups); and the Sarcee and Gros Ventres peoples (allies of the Blackfeet).

Old Man told the five tribes that their territory in the northern Great Plains (present-day Montana in the United States and Saskatchewan in Canada) was meant for them alone. He warned them to let no one else live on their land—especially white people—or they would lose everything.

This is one story the Blackfeet Indians tell to explain how they came to be. In another version, Creator Sun makes the world and provides the people with everything they need. In still another version, Napi is able to take the form of Creator Sun or Old Man. This is why some Blackfeet tell the creation myth of Old Man but still refer to the sun as Creator Sun.

It is not surprising that they have so many different—but compatible—beliefs, since the Blackfeet Indians are actually made up of three distinct tribes: the Siksika (the first Blackfeet), the Kainah (Many Chiefs) or Blood, and the Peigan, Piegan, or Pikuni (Poorly Dressed Ones). The first white explorers in Blackfeet territory probably thought these Indians belonged to one tribe since they all spoke the same language and lived in the same way. The three groups were collectively named the Blackfeet by outsiders because the soles of their moccasins were black.

The Blackfeet roamed the prairies of their native land on foot until around 1700, when

Even before the arrival of horses, the Blackfeet had managed to thrive in an environment that featured rugged mountains, expansive prairies, and wildly variable weather conditions.

they started using horses, which had been brought to America by Spanish *conquistadores* in the 1500s. On horseback, the Blackfeet expanded their territory—and struck fear into the hearts of anyone foolish enough to trespass on their land.

It is unclear how long the Blackfeet lived in the northern Plains region before the arrival of horses. Historians believe that their ancestors—like those of all Native Americans—

walked over a land bridge that once stretched across the Bering Sea and connected present-day Siberia to Alaska. This walk across the Bering Strait may have happened 30,000 or more years ago.

The northern Plains certainly tested the mettle of the first Blackfeet who lived there. The region is extremely cold in winter, hot in summer, and prone to flash floods and hailstorms. But the land also offered the Blackfeet abundant prey such as mink, fox, and bear.

Of all the plants and animals given to the Blackfeet by Old Man, the people treasured the buffalo most of all. The buffalo's immense size and sharp horns, however, made hunting them extremely dangerous.

But the Blackfeet's most important food source was the buffalo, which once roamed the Great Plains in herds large enough to cover an entire horizon. Whether they were hunting on foot before the 18th century or on horseback at the height of their power during the 19th century, the Blackfeet were always thankful for the buffalo, or American bison. These animals were the greatest gift Old Man had given them at the beginning of time. ▲

Buffalo were such a vital source of food and clothing to the Blackfeet that the Indians developed ingenious methods of capturing them. These tricks included setting controlled brush fires, causing stampedes, and even disguising themselves as wolves in order to sneak up on grazing herds (shown here).

CHAPTER 2

Of Buffalo and Elk Dogs

There was no animal more important to the Blackfeet than the American bison, or buffalo. Before white hunters came to the Great Plains, millions of buffalo roamed freely from the Rocky Mountains all the way to the eastern woodlands. So vital were the buffalo to the Blackfeet that Old Man made them before creating any other animal. Their usefulness earned them a special Blackfeet name: *eye-i-in-nawhw,* or "shall be peeled (skinned)."

The Blackfeet let no part of the buffalo go to waste: in addition to eating the meat, the people used the skins, the horns, and even the dried dung of the animals (as fuel for fires). The humps, tongues, and livers of buffalo were Blackfeet delicacies.

The hide was every bit as important as the meat was to the Indians' survival. Buffalo leather was the raw material for those black-soled moccasins that gave the tribe its very name. The people also used leather to make *breechcloths*, leggings, dresses, and robes. Tougher, untanned skins (rawhide) were suitable for making sturdy ropes, unbreakable shields, and envelope-shaped bags called *parfleches*. The Blackfeet knew how to waterproof buffalo hides: they carefully smoked the hides over a flame until they were ideal for making *tepees* that would stay dry in soaking rains.

In addition to hides, the Blackfeet used buffalo bones, horns, hooves, and hair to make utensils, arrowheads, jewelry, and children's toys. The cleaned lining of a buffalo's stomach made a fine water carrier. To the Blackfeet, the animal was a gift from Creator Sun, proof that the people were loved and cared for. To waste any part of a kill would be both foolish and sinful.

Just as the Blackfeet's physical lives depended on the buffalo, so did their religious practices. Hunters thought buffalo had *supernatural* powers. They usually avoided killing

This Blackfeet man stands in front of two buffalo-hide tepees with his horse. The watertight, decorated tepees are evidence of the buffalo's almost unlimited usefulness, and the horse is a sign of wealth as well as an asset on the hunt.

old animals and sought four-year-old calves, which were prized for their tender meat and supple hides. The people believed that these special buffalo (and all animals) could only be caught if they themselves permitted it to happen. Therefore, Blackfeet holy people prayed to the buffalo in order to thank them for their sacrifices and to ask for continued success in the hunt. Holy men also used magic to attract the buffalo, performing rituals with sacred objects made from buffalo bones. Many important Blackfeet religious ceremonies required buffalo skulls. *Medicine bundles*, carried by individuals for protection and power, always included some part of the buffalo.

The Blackfeet's worship of the buffalo was at least partly inspired by the animals' tremendous size and power. Hunters on foot faced the danger of being trampled by these massive animals, which weigh about 2,000 pounds, stand roughly six feet tall at the shoulder, and tend to stampede when frightened. Buffalo also have a good sense of smell. To the Indians, this meant that they had to stay downwind of their prey and wear little clothing on the hunt. Otherwise, the buffalo would quickly smell human scent and stampede.

Stripped down to their breechcloths and armed only with bows and arrows, the Blackfeet relied on teamwork to feed and clothe themselves. Everything they did to attract and kill the buffalo was a group effort. In fact, hunting alone was considered a crime. Although one or two hunters might bring a bison down, their solo hunting would cause the rest of the herd to stampede—and make it impossible for anybody else to get food. Sharing was such a part of Blackfeet life that some young unmarried men had the special honor of giving their kill to widows or to elderly people who had nobody else to hunt for them.

Women and children shared in the work, too. Long before the hunt began, the entire group would try to lure the buffalo close to camp by burning old, tough prairie grass every spring so that younger, tastier grass would grow in its place.

Once the hunt was under way, a few men might sneak up on the herd, disguised as wolves or as female buffalo. Their human identity concealed, they could sit quietly among the herd without frightening the buffalo. The hunters waited for an animal to stray from the herd so that they could overpower it without scaring the other buffalo.

Another method of hunting involved the whole tribe, killed more buffalo at once, and took advantage of the buffalo's poor eyesight. People and their dogs would run up behind a herd—causing it to stampede in panic—and would then drive the animals over a cliff to their death. Some cliffs were used for this purpose for thousands of years: one cliff near present-day Alberta, Canada, is known to this day as Head-Smashed-In Buffalo Jump. This style of hunting worked for the Blackfeet because the tall grass of the Great Plains hides steep slopes on the horizon—and because buffalo have very poor vision. Also, this method did not require horses in order to be successful.

For the Blackfeet who hunted far from the Rocky Mountains, cliffs were harder to find. They constructed wooden corrals on the prairie called *piskuns*. The Indians stampeded the buffalo into these large wooden enclosures, then shot them with their arrows. An especially elaborate piskun would also have a sort of raised bridge leading into the corral so that the buffalo would fall and injure themselves as they landed in the trap.

Properly dressing the freshly killed buffalo was vital. Blackfeet women went to work right in the field—skinning, cleaning, and cutting the kill into pieces small enough to carry back to camp. The Blackfeet used sleigh-like carriers called *travois*, which they tied to the backs of their dogs, to transport buffalo meat.

But by the mid-1700s, the Blackfeet had discovered an even better pack animal than the dog. Spanish explorers first brought horses to the Southwest in 1541, but it wasn't until around 1770 that they became a central part of Blackfeet life. Like other Great Plains tribes, the Blackfeet quickly learned to ride like born horsemen. They also began to breed small, agile Indian ponies. These sturdy horses became important as items of trade, as gifts, and as symbols of wealth.

Indian ponies also helped make their owners rich in food and clothing. Buffalo hunting —although still dangerous—was safer and faster on horseback. Horses could also carry more butchered meat than dogs could. Hence, they were called Big Dogs or Elk Dogs. Once the people hitched horses to their travois, they could migrate from place to place more easily than ever.

The Blackfeet weren't the only Indians who had discovered the value of the horse, however. They always had to guard against horse raids by enemy tribes. When a Blackfeet warrior feared that horse thieves were near, his favorite pony would sleep in the tepee with him while his wife slept outside! Horses changed Blackfeet culture dramatically: boys could now prove their manhood by raiding horses from neighboring tribes. Indeed, the bravado of young horse thieves sometimes started wars —much to the dismay of older Blackfeet men.

It seems fitting that one explanation of how people first captured and tamed horses is a myth about a young man who needed to prove himself. The Blackfeet tell the story of Long Arrow, an orphan who was always treated as an outcast by his tribe even though he was a fine hunter and a brave man. He wanted to earn his people's respect once and for all.

Long Arrow told his adoptive father, Good Running, that he wanted to do something great to win the tribe's esteem. Good Running told him about a people living at the bottom of a faraway lake who kept beasts that were as large as elk but as tame as dogs. These creatures were called *po-no-kah-mita,* or Elk Dogs. Although many had gone in search of the Elk Dogs, none had ever returned.

Unafraid, Long Arrow traveled south until he came to a pond. The pond spirit rose from the water, taking the form of a man, and spoke to him. It said that if Long Arrow rode four times four days and spoke to the pond spirit's uncle, then the Elk Dogs would be his. Long Arrow rode for 16 harrowing days until he reached a large lake. Out came a giant lake spirit, who tried to frighten the young man. When it realized that Long Arrow wasn't easily frightened, the spirit led him to another magic lake—at the bottom of which lived the Elk Dogs.

The story of Long Arrow illustrates the high regard the Blackfeet had for horses. Horses surpassed dogs at pulling travois because they were strong enough to carry tons of food and supplies—as well as young passengers—over great distances.

Exhausted from weeks of searching, Long Arrow fell asleep at the magic lake's edge. He awoke to find a small boy standing over him. The boy told Long Arrow to follow him to the bottom of the lake. Long Arrow dove in—and discovered that not only could he breathe underwater, but the water did not even wet

him. The boy's grandfather, a powerful magician, awaited them at the bottom. He shared a pipe with the young warrior, and showed him the fabled Elk Dogs.

Then the boy revealed a secret: anyone who saw the old man's feet could ask for a gift. It wasn't until a few days later that Long Arrow managed to sneak a glimpse of the old magician's feet. The young man discovered that they were actually hooves, just like the Elk Dogs' feet. Realizing that Long Arrow had learned his secret, the old man granted him three wishes. Long Arrow asked for the old man's belt, his medicine robe, and some Elk Dogs.

The old man agreed and showed Long Arrow how to use his new gifts: the robe was worn to sneak up on the Elk Dogs, and wearing the belt would teach Long Arrow their songs and prayers. Once an outcast, Long Arrow now had not only the Elk Dogs, but also the magic to tame them. He returned to his village, a hero at last, with the horses trailing behind him.

Like Long Arrow himself, the Blackfeet found their lives completely transformed after they tamed the horse. Doing so allowed them to live a life that was more *nomadic* than ever, riding freely from place to place. It made hunting easier. This in turn meant that people had better nourishment and clothing than ever before. Horses changed the Blackfeet into a people of prosperity, mobility, and military power. ▲

CHAPTER 3

Blackfeet Culture

Tradition was the most important ingredient of Blackfeet culture. How the people dressed and worshiped, what they ate, and who they married were all determined by what their elders had done before them. Because they had an *oral tradition* instead of a written language, they learned about the past from old people's stories or from what they could observe themselves.

The Blackfeet recorded events in picture form rather than in written accounts. This man paints pictographs on a hide.

This does not mean that the Blackfeet were unable to adapt to change in the world around them, though. One event to which they adjusted superbly was the arrival of horses. The story of Long Arrow and the Elk Dogs shows that the Blackfeet realized how useful horses could be, and took action to obtain them.

It is hard to overstate how much horsemanship changed the Blackfeet social world. It transformed the related tribes into a major military nation. Blackfeet warriors interviewed by *anthropologists* around the turn of this century could recall instances of being at war with up to 10 enemy tribes at once. Stealing horses from rival tribes enabled young men to gain both status and wealth. Older Blackfeet leaders found peace agreements with other tribes difficult to enforce because so many younger men sought the prestige that came with a successful horse raid. Sometimes young Blackfeet horse thieves ignored the authority of the older men entirely and formed breakaway bands of their own.

The flexible nature of leadership in Blackfeet society made the formation of new bands possible. A tribe had no single chief. People became leaders if they had special skills. Leaders were generally expected to be outstanding hunters, warriors, or religious figures. They were also expected to be good-hearted and generous.

There were peace chiefs and war chiefs. War chiefs were expected to defend the tribe against rivals, to distinguish themselves in battle, and to gain wealth and honor for the group by raiding the peoples they conquered. When a war chief's strength declined with age, he simply retired and let a promising young fighter take his place.

Peace chiefs, on the other hand, were expected to maintain harmony within the tribe. Although they had to be brave like the war chiefs, they were less concerned about military glory. The peace chiefs settled disputes between people, kept order, and set an example of fairness and dignity for the rest of the tribe. Peace chiefs also recorded the Winter Count, an annual record of important events in the community. Sometimes, the chiefs illustrated the year's events in *pictographs*, which they painted on hides. Most Winter Counts, however, were verbal records carefully memorized by the peace chiefs.

One thing chiefs never did was administer justice. This was done by someone the whole group appointed to order punishments for wrongdoers. This judge made sure that a punishment was carried out by a special council or by the victim's family. Crimes against other people could be punishable by death; petty crimes such as theft were dealt with by shaming the thief and returning stolen property.

A child growing up in a Blackfeet band saw the consequences of bad behavior and learned to be a disciplined member of his or her community. As soon as they were able, children accompanied their mothers to the field after a buffalo kill to clean, skin, and butcher the carcasses. Girls prepared for adulthood by watching their mothers. Blackfeet women made clothing and shelter for their families out of buffalo hides. They were also in charge of breaking down and reassembling the tepees every time the group moved. The women also developed many different ways of cooking the game that the men killed. One buffalo dish was a sort of sausage made by cleaning the intestines, stuffing them with meat and herbs, and then cooking them over a fire. Women also gathered berries and vegetables such as wild peas and prairie turnips to balance the people's diet.

In addition to buffalo, the men hunted quail, deer, pronghorn, and rabbit. They did not fish, however: historians believe that the tribe had a *taboo* against eating fish. Nor did the Blackfeet farm any crop other than tobacco. Instead, they got beans, squash, corn and pumpkins through trade with the nearby Mandan and Pawnee peoples.

Because men and women generally excelled at different things, they needed each other in order to survive on the Great Plains. It was Old Man who first brought men and

continued on page 41

A HERITAGE ENDURES THROUGH ART

Before the coming of whites, the Blackfeet decorated their clothing, tepees, tools, and medicine bundles. They adorned both sacred and everyday items with feathers, fur, elk teeth, vegetable dyes, and porcupine quills. The first white traders to Blackfeet territory brought glass beads and brass ornaments—and gave the Indians new ways to enhance their already-vibrant designs.

But the coming of whites also heralded the end of the Blackfeet's nomadic way of life. After they had been forced onto reservations, many Blackfeet turned their attention to beadwork and crafts. As a result, their headdresses, clothes, and accessories became increasingly ornate during the early reservation years.

A woman's leather purse, decorated with small glass beads. The Blackfeet commonly decorated objects with large triangle, hourglass, or diamond designs composed of many small squares.

A girl's hide dress with an ornately decorated yoke. The beads on this dress were sewn in such a way that they resemble porcupine quill designs.

This woman's dress was made from two elk skins sewn together so that the hind quarters formed sleeves. The yoke is overlaid with beads and fringed with brass-colored beads and cowrie shells.

A swept-back or Sioux-style eagle feather headdress, decorated with beads and weasel pelts.
The red and yellow tassels on the end of each eagle feather are wisps of dyed horse hair,
glued to the feathers with lime plaster. This style of headdress was adopted by the Blackfeet
from other Plains tribes in the mid-1890s and could be worn by almost anyone.

A stand-up or Blackfeet-style headdress decorated with weasel pelts and brass upholstery tacks. This type of headdress, which could only be worn by exceptional warriors, apparently originated with the Blackfeet and was believed to have magical powers.

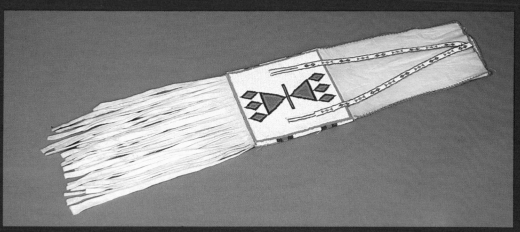

This Blackfeet tobacco pouch was probably used to carry kinnikinnick, a pipe, and other smoking utensils. Similar pouches were carried by members of almost all Plains tribes.

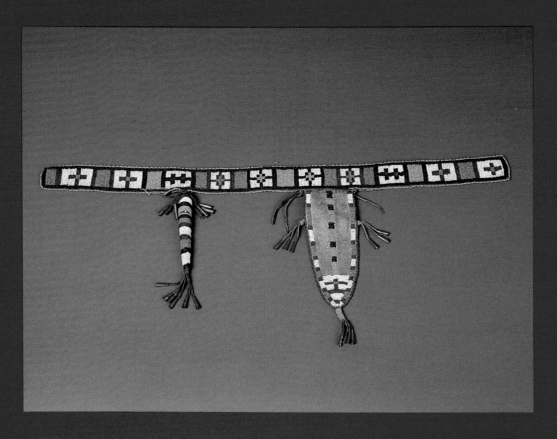

A beaded leather belt with two pouches, a narrow one carrying an awl and wider one for carrying a knife. Metal knives, introduced by white traders, quickly became popular among the Blackfeet, and Blackfeet artisans fashioned many different types of knife sheaths.

Another beaded leather knife sheath, shaped like a beaver.

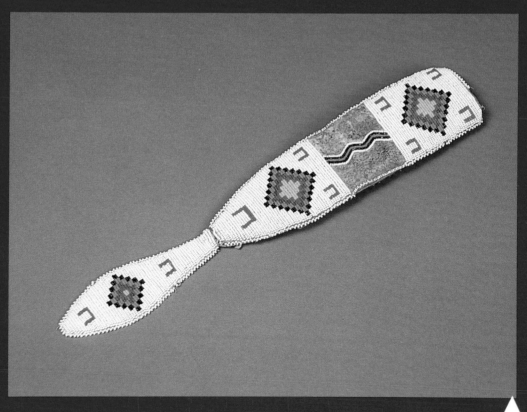

An ornately beaded bodice, beaded to resemble porcupine quills. The bead fringe is decorated with brass bells and cowrie shells.

continued from page 32

women together. According to Blackfeet myth, shortly after their creation, the men were naked because they were unable to tan buffalo hides. The women were starving because they were poor hunters. Old Man made them agree to do different jobs so that they could help each other.

A Blackfeet marriage could take place after a young man had proven himself in battle or on a horse raid. He then sent a trusted friend or relative to his intended bride's home with a gift of horses. If she accepted the horses, the couple was engaged. The wedding was usually a few days later. Little is known about the actual ceremony, but some accounts say that the fingers of the bride and groom were cut and their blood was mingled to seal the marriage. After a feast to honor the new couple, the wife left her family's tepee to join her husband.

Because their culture encouraged men to risk their lives in battle, many Blackfeet males died young. This might have been one reason that the tribe practiced polygamy (marriage between a man and two or more wives). Young women often married men who were in their late thirties or older. These older husbands no longer needed to rush into battle to prove themselves, so they were available to their wives and children. In addition, life was easier for women if they could share their many chores with other wives.

Some Blackfeet women made reputations for themselves as warriors, however. Blackfeet culture occasionally permitted men and women to step outside of their traditional roles. The most famous female warrior was named Running Eagle. She began her military career after her husband was killed in a raid against the Crow people. Running Eagle led war parties for many years. She was even admitted to the Brave Dogs, the most prestigious Blackfeet warrior society. Running Eagle continued to distinguish herself in battle until she was killed while fighting the Flathead tribe in 1860.

Perhaps the last great female Blackfeet warrior was a young wife named Throwing Down, who went out on war raids with her husband, Weasel Tail, during the 1880s. She reportedly did this because she adored her husband and wanted to watch over him. The birth of her first child forced Throwing Down to give up warfare for motherhood, however.

The Blackfeet people created a world in which a person's status within the tribe was determined by his or her abilities and personal qualities. They also taught their children and grandchildren tribal traditions against the backdrop of a changing environment. The people

Weasel Tail was an esteemed Blackfeet warrior during the late 1800s. His wife, Throwing Down, worried so much about his safety that she joined him in battle.

created social customs that preserved order within their communities. It was their ability to adjust to change, plus their spiritual beliefs, that allowed the Blackfeet to rejoice in all of the good things that the world around them had to offer. ▲

CHAPTER 4

Thanking the Creator

Blackfeet culture and religion were inseparable. All of the people's activities, from hunting to raising their children, were infused with their spiritual beliefs. These beliefs governed their cultural traditions. All Blackfeet children underwent spiritual *rites of passage* as they grew into adulthood. Religion was not confined to just these ceremonies, or to the weekly day of worship observed by many modern faiths. Instead, every day was filled with prayers and offerings to the spirit world.

One reason for this was the Blackfeet's belief that all plants and animals—and even non-

A Blackfeet man pauses to watch the setting sun. The sun is an object of special reverence in traditional Blackfeet religion.

living things—possessed spiritual energy. The people felt that all things on earth were their relatives, since everything had one creator. This meant that even a simple act like picking berries involved giving thanks to the plant for sharing its fruit. If a person forgot to give thanks, he or she feared that starvation for the entire tribe would result.

Animals commanded respect, too. The Blackfeet assured themselves of continued success in the hunt by praying to animal spirits. In addition to the buffalo, the people considered wolves and bears sacred. Wolves were admired for their great cunning; warriors donned wolfskin clothing, hoping it would make them smart and alert in battle. Bears, like buffalo, were revered because they were so powerful that few other animals dared to attack them.

The forces of nature also had special powers. The wind relayed messages from the creator to the people. Some Blackfeet were thought to have the ability to hear the creator's words on the breeze. North, south, east, west, earth, and sky—the six directions—were each believed to have unique powers. East was the most important direction, however, because it was home to the rising sun.

The sun was the Blackfeet's central object of worship. They held their most important religious ceremony to honor it. The Sun Dance usually took place in late spring or early summer when the moon was full. So elaborate were the preparations that it was only performed once a year.

Getting the people ready for a Sun Dance fell to the tribal *shamans*. These people could interpret messages from the spirit world. They used their powers to heal the sick when the herbal medicines made by Blackfeet doctors failed. Some shamans could also predict the future. One of their most important jobs, however, was to prepare and bless the tribal medicine bundles for the Sun Dance. These bundles contained special charms (a lock of bear fur to give the people strength, for example).

Shamans were just as important to the tribe as war and peace chiefs, but while the chiefs were almost always men, any woman who demonstrated special powers could become a shaman. Tribal holy women were very important among the Blackfeet: the Sun Dance could only be sponsored by a woman.

The woman who sponsored the Sun Dance was called the Sacred Woman of the Dance. If she had prayed to the sun for something important (such as the recovery of a sick child) and received it during the previous year, she would host the dance to express her grati-

tude. Sun Dance festivities could last for up
to a month: during that time, the Sacred Woman
wore a special headdress, dress, and robe.
She was treated with the utmost respect. She

was also expected to give away several horses and other valuable gifts. Because serving as the Sacred Woman was expensive, people only did it to repay extremely important favors.

The same was true of the dancers themselves. Men were the only ones who actually performed the Sun Dance, but not all men did it every year. Only those who had something very important to give thanks for danced.

This was in part because the Sun Dance demanded every bit of strength that a man could muster. After a period of prayer and fasting, everyone would come to a specially built Sun Lodge, which had a pole in the middle of the dance floor. Each dancer would wear a beaded necklace and a loincloth that hung down to his ankles. When his turn to dance came, the skin of the man's chest or back was pierced with a wooden stick; this stick was tied to the center lodgepole with a long rope. While tethered to the pole, the man would dance around it, his body straining against the rope until the stick tore through his skin and he was freed. The pieces of flesh that were torn from the dancers' bodies were left on the sticks and offered to Creator Sun.

Completing the Sun Dance without fainting was an amazing feat. To distract themselves from their pain, the dancers would focus on

This shaman wears a bear costume to perform a healing ritual. The Blackfeet allowed both men and women of great spiritual power to become shamans.

the medicine bundle that was tied to the top of the center pole. Any visions that came to them while dancing were considered especially sacred.

Visions from the spirit world were important sources of guidance for people of all

Blackfeet women build a Sun Dance lodge. Women made great contributions to the religious life of their communities. In fact, only women were permitted to host Sun Dance ceremonies.

ages. Blackfeet youths, for instance, were recognized as adult tribe members after undergoing a ceremony called the *vision quest*. When a boy was ready, he would seek the advice of elders on how to conduct his quest. Then, he fasted and went into a *sweat lodge* to ritually cleanse himself.

Now fully prepared in body and mind, the vision seeker would find a place far from camp and wait for the spirit world to contact him. The wait usually lasted four days, during which he would go without food, water, or shelter. If his vision quest was successful, the boy would receive a sign from the spirits: he might hear a message on the wind, encounter a wolf, or spot a flash of lightning in the sky. Whatever the young man saw or heard would become his personal symbol and guide (somewhat like a guardian angel, which many people believe in today). He would add a symbol of the vision to his personal medicine bundle. Before going on the hunt or into battle, he might also paint a picture of his new spirit guide on his body.

Because Blackfeet culture valued women as much as it did men, girls could go on vision quests, too. The visions experienced by young women were considered no less important than those of young men. One difference between male and female vision seekers was that girls usually did not travel far from camp on their vision quests.

Vision quests and Sun Dances were dramatic events that took a lot of preparation. The Blackfeet also strengthened their ties to the spirit world through the smoking of tobacco—which could be done privately or as part of tribal ceremonies. Tobacco was so important to the Blackfeet that it was the only crop they actually farmed.

They planted the tobacco amid elaborate songs and ceremonies, then abandoned the seedlings until they were ready for harvest (magical beings were believed to care for the plants as they grew). Once it was harvested, however, it was used in virtually all Blackfeet ceremonies. A mixture of tobacco and tree barks, called *kinnikinnick*, was smoked in a special pipe called a *calumet* to seal peace treaties. But a smoker could also use tobacco by himself for his own purposes: to attract game, to scare away evil spirits, or to seek a blessing.

To the Blackfeet Indians, religion and culture were often the same thing: to grow up in Blackfeet culture, children had to undergo a fixed set of rituals, since the people practiced only one religion. That faith was a set of spiritual beliefs that called for public ceremonies of thanksgiving and sacrifice as well as pri-

A dancer tests his strength and courage during a Sun Dance ceremony in 1892. The dancer's flesh was pierced; he was then tied to a lodge pole from which he tried to pull free. This painful ritual was a way of giving thanks to the sun for the past year's blessings.

vate prayers to appease the nature spirits, which were everywhere. The Blackfeet lived safely in their social and religious world until the early 1800s—when their lives were forever changed by the arrival of strangers in their homeland. ▲

CHAPTER 5

Lords of the Plains

The eight Blackfeet horse raiders encountered by Meriwether Lewis in the early 1800s may have resembled the warrior in this picture. The Blackfeet used the horses and guns introduced by Europeans to their advantage, but they also suffered great losses after their first contact with whites.

The years 1750–1850 were the glory days of traditional Blackfeet life. By 1750, they had mastered the horse; most bands had acquired large herds by raiding other tribes and by breeding their own stock. The Blackfeet enjoyed easier hunting, increased military might, and great mobility until a large number of white settlers came to Montana and southern Canada during the 1850s.

A few Europeans had visited the northern Plains before 1850, however. By the early 1600s, Spanish explorers had ridden into the Great Plains, giving Indians their first glimpse of horses. These men probably had some contact with the Blackfeet. The first American explorer to meet them was Meriwether Lewis. President Thomas Jefferson had sent him and William Clark to explore the Louisiana Purchase, a huge stretch of land that America had bought from France. Lewis and Clark's journey lasted from 1804 to 1806. At one point, the two men split up near the Rocky Mountains. Lewis and a party of four other men were attacked by eight Blackfeet horse raiders. Although outnumbered, Lewis' party managed to kill two of the raiders and take their horses.

Most early meetings between whites and the Blackfeet were unfriendly. One member of the Lewis and Clark expedition, a trapper named John Colter, decided to stay behind when the others went home. Colter narrowly escaped death as a prisoner of the Blackfeet. His partner in the fur trade, John Potts, was not so lucky: terrified, Potts tried to escape, shooting one of his Indian captors. He was killed. The outraged warriors decided to kill Colter as well. They took his clothes and shoes and chased him across the prairie as they tried to spear him. Colter outran them and kept running—traveling 300 miles in one week.

Colter—and other British and American trappers who came to Blackfeet territory—

angered the tribe in many ways. First, they traded with enemy tribes, such as the Crow and the Flathead. These tribes could now obtain well-made guns, with which they fought the Blackfeet. Second, whites nearly trapped the beaver population to extinction, depriving the Indians of pelts. Finally, they hunted buffalo wastefully (only taking the tastiest parts and the hides) and upset the animals' migration patterns by building settlements.

The discovery of gold in the Rocky Mountains during the 1850s only worsened the Indians' situation. A flood of white settlers began to overrun Blackfeet territory. Gold miners grazed their horses and cattle on the Plains. Some picked fights with the Indians they encountered.

The Blackfeet did not watch idly as their land was confiscated and the buffalo were killed in droves. They fought back. White settlers feared the Blackfeet more than they did most other tribes. They began to demand the protection of the United States government. The first treaty between the United States and the Blackfeet was the Treaty of Fort Laramie in 1851. The tribe ignored it because they were never consulted about its terms, nor were they present when it was signed.

Lamed Bull's Treaty of 1855 was the first agreement that both sides signed. It stated that the Blackfeet would give up half of their hunting land. They were also expected to allow Americans to live in their territory, and to allow railroads and telegraph lines to go through it. In return, the Blackfeet were promised $20,000 per year in food and supplies. The government pledged to spend another $15,000 each year to school them and to convert them to Christianity.

Relations between the whites and the Blackfeet improved for a short time. Then whites began to use the treaty unfairly. They gave the tribe payments in the form of stale food, shabby blankets, and—worst of all—alcohol. The Indians were forced to rely on poor government food as the buffalo grew increasingly scarce. Betrayed, they renewed their attacks on white settlers.

Soon, battles between the Blackfeet and whites became so frequent that the settlers asked the government for help. On January 6, 1870, that help came in the form of the United States Cavalry, led by Colonel E. M. Baker. Baker unleashed a surprise attack on a camp of Peigan Blackfeet, killing approximately 200 Indians in a matter of minutes. The band that Baker's men attacked was made up of mostly women, children, and old people. When it was also discovered that this band was innocent of any raids against whites, the so-called Peigan War was quickly renamed the Baker Massacre.

Baker's victims were especially defenseless because they had just suffered a smallpox outbreak that had taken many lives. Contagious diseases killed more Blackfeet than did warfare. Like all Native Americans, they had never been exposed to viruses like smallpox, chicken pox, and influenza until Europeans came to America. An illness that merely sickened a white person could easily kill an Indian. In 1837, for instance, smallpox wiped out roughly two-thirds of the entire Blackfeet population.

Already faced with deadly diseases and the loss of the buffalo, the Blackfeet living in America also struggled to hold on to their land. The United States government rewrote treaties to make Blackfeet territory smaller. This made the South Peigan of Montana increasingly dependent on government food rations. In the winter of 1883–84, there were hardly any buffalo left in Montana. The government did not provide the Indians with food—even though rations were promised to them in a treaty. The resulting deaths of more than 600 Blackfeet men, women, and children caused that time to be known as Starvation Winter.

Starvation Winter so devastated the South Peigan Blackfeet that they could no longer

fight for their land. In 1887, the General Allotment Act confined all Blackfeet living in the United States to a *reservation* in Montana.

The Blackfeet living in Canada fared slightly better than their American counterparts. The Kainah Blackfeet, for instance, had consented to live on a reserve (the Canadian name for a reservation) in 1877. Even so, the end of the 19th century found Blackfeet in both countries reduced to powerlessness. They once rode freely over a vast domain: now, they sat waiting on reservations for government food that seldom arrived as promised. ▲

Canadian Blackfeet chiefs pose with two officials (second row) in 1884. Red Crow, head chief of the Kainahs, stands between them. The removal of Canadian Blackfeet to the reserves went somewhat more smoothly than that of their American counterparts to the Montana reservation.

CHAPTER 6

Building a Future

By the end of the 1800s, it appeared that the Blackfeet were indeed losing everything, just as Old Man had predicted long ago. In 1898, the United States Congress passed the Curtis Act. The Curtis Act attempted to force Native Americans in the United States to accept *allotments* whether they wanted to or not. After their lands were split up, Indians were subject to American laws and taxes; their tribal governments were ignored or dismantled.

The South Peigan in Montana escaped allotments because they had signed a treaty with the United States government in 1895

Despite past pressure from the U.S. and Canadian governments to abandon their traditional culture, Blackfeet children of today are taught to treasure their native heritage. These Kainah children stand in front of a play tepee made from flour sacks.

which stated that the reservation would never be split into allotments without their consent. But other provisions of the Curtis Act still pressured them to live like whites. The Sun Dance, the Blackfeet's most important religious ceremony, was now against the law. So was the wearing of long hair by men. This rule was hard on the Blackfeet, whose men traditionally took great pride in their hair, treating it with bear fat to make it shine.

Blackfeet children were affected by the Curtis Act most of all. Newborn babies were no longer supposed to be given tribal names. As children grew up, they were forbidden from learning Blackfeet traditions from tribal elders. To ensure that they would grow up to be English-speaking Christians, the government established schools both on and off reservations. Children were sometimes kidnapped from their homes and sent to boarding schools, where they would be punished if caught singing tribal songs or doing tribal dances.

Some schools were less harsh but no less intent on turning the Indians into Christians. Religious orders, especially the Jesuits, established missions and private schools on the Blackfeet reservation. The Jesuit priests, called Black Robes by the Indians because of their attire, succeeded in converting some Black-

Siksika Blackfeet children at a mission school in 1892. Although the Christian founders of such schools usually meant well, their students were often severely punished for observing traditional Blackfeet customs.

feet to Catholicism. Other branches of Christianity also founded churches on Blackfeet land. Christian missionaries considered traditional Blackfeet religion evil because it was based upon nature spirits instead of God and Jesus Christ.

Even so, religious leaders who lived among the Blackfeet were often kinder to them than government agents were. The Bureau of Indian Affairs (BIA) was the branch of the federal government that supervised reservation life. Indian agents from the BIA often treated the Indians like children. For example, Blackfeet adults were not allowed to leave the Montana reservation without permission from an Indian agent or to receive outside visitors who didn't have a pass.

Indian agents believed that such restrictions would prevent Native Americans of dif-

By 1911, the year this U.S. government poster advertised cheap Indian land, reservation life had left many Native Americans desperately poor. The General Allotment Act of 1887 had resulted in Indians selling off vast amounts of tribal land for very little money.

INDIAN LAND FOR SALE

GET A HOME
OF
YOUR OWN
❋
EASY PAYMENTS

PERFECT TITLE
❋
POSSESSION
WITHIN
THIRTY DAYS

FINE LANDS IN THE WEST

IRRIGATED IRRIGABLE　　**GRAZING**　　**AGRICULTURAL DRY FARMING**

IN 1910 THE DEPARTMENT OF THE INTERIOR SOLD UNDER SEALED BIDS ALLOTTED INDIAN LAND AS FOLLOWS:

ferent tribes from banding together to fight whites. They also thought it would stop the spread of traditional Indian beliefs and practices. In addition to compelling the Blackfeet to imitate the dress and appearance of whites, both the United States and Canadian governments prompted the tribes to give up their portable tepees for permanent wooden houses. Unfortunately, these structures were usually tiny and run-down.

Although they funded efforts to make the Blackfeet live like white Europeans, both the United States and Canada spent very little on health care for them. As a result, many Blackfeet in both countries were malnourished. They also suffered from tuberculosis and trachoma (an eye infection that can lead to blindness) in large numbers.

The Indians often went hungry because of their inability to grow enough food. The United States and Canadian governments both made some poorly funded efforts to "teach" the Blackfeet agriculture. Not surprisingly, farming was a failure for the Indians in America and Canada alike. The tribes on both sides of the border were succeeding at cattle ranching, though. The grassy Plains were better suited to this than to farming, and the Blackfeet proved to be excellent herders. But neither the Canadian nor the American Indians were allowed to manage their herds without government supervision. Many of the government cattle managers were unskilled themselves, and their interference frustrated the Blackfeet.

Still worse, the United States government violated its treaty with the Blackfeet in 1907, when it passed the Blackfeet Allotment Act without the Indians' consent. The Montana reservation was broken into allotments—and roughly 800,000 "extra" acres were sold to whites. The parcels of land assigned to individual families were now too small to graze cattle on. The South Peigan of Montana were forced to give up the only way of life that had held any promise for them since being forced onto a reservation.

After several years, Native Americans were permitted to sell their allotments. Poor and frustrated in their efforts to farm, many Blackfeet were convinced by corrupt whites to sell their land at very low prices. The Indians were swindled in other ways, too. To get allotment land, some whites went so far as to become the legal guardians of Indian children who stood to inherit it.

World War I came in 1917, bringing some temporary improvements to reservation life. Young Blackfeet men eager to fight for the American and Canadian armed forces were

A Blackfeet man shows his son a traditional pipe. Interest in learning about and preserving traditional Native American culture has grown in the United States over the last 30 years.

at first turned away. As the war dragged on, however, a few were recruited, and they served well in Europe.

The most important Blackfeet contribution to World War I came in the form of a drive to make the Montana reservation into a productive farming zone. In contrast to earlier efforts to farm, Blackfeet agriculture programs during World War I were a success. The farmers worked hard, and their economy grew. Unfortunately, this success was short-lived. During the war, white agents on the Kainah Blackfeet reserve in Canada were given complete control over the Indians' cattle. So many head of Kainah cattle died from neglect during the winter of 1919–20 that the Indians faced financial ruin.

In part to thank Native Americans for their efforts during World War I, the United States government granted them full citizenship in 1924. This wouldn't happen in Canada until 1960. But the South Peigan Blackfeet living in Montana were still poor, as were most reservation Indians. It was clear that the BIA's close supervision was doing the Indians more harm than good.

In 1934, the United States Congress passed the Indian Reorganization Act (IRA). The IRA restored power to tribal governments on reservations. The South Peigan went to work immediately: they founded the Blackfeet Business Council and drafted a tribal constitution in 1935. In 1937, they built a new hospital on the reservation. Funds for tribal schools were also provided under the IRA—freeing the Indians to teach their children the old traditions once more.

When America became involved in World War II, many Blackfeet men and women served in the United States Armed Forces. Others did manufacturing work in defense plants away from the Montana reservation. For a while, the South Peigan enjoyed the security of regular paychecks. After the war, however, white and black workers came back to their jobs. Upon returning to the reservation, the Indians faced poverty again. This prompted many Blackfeet to leave the reservation permanently in search of work. If they were lucky enough to land jobs, their work was often low-paying and they were frequently mistreated by non-Indians. By the 1950s, many Blackfeet workers had moved back to the reservation.

The 1950s also ushered in the idea of *termination*. The BIA wanted to cut off rations, payments, and services to Native Americans. They instructed tribes to prepare "termination plans." Many groups refused to do so. Since reservations often held very little opportunity

for employment, the United States government wound up spending more on assistance
to terminated tribes than it had when the tribes
were funded by the BIA. The end of the 1950s

The old meets the new: a sprinkling of automobiles (right) blends in with the horses and the tepees at the Siksika Blackfeet's 1943 Sun Dance festival.

was also the end of termination policies.

Although the Blackfeet had been free to teach their children traditional culture for an entire generation now, few young people could speak the Blackfeet language. Elders who could speak Blackfeet fluently were dying without passing on their knowledge. But the 1960s and 1970s were marked by an increased sense of Native American pride. Native Americans formed intertribal (made up of many tribes) groups and began to fight for better treatment by their governments. Individually, the Blackfeet and other tribes turned their attention toward preserving their languages, religions, and customs.

Today, the Blackfeet realize that in order to preserve and promote their tribal traditions, they must tackle some difficult problems. They currently battle high rates of alcoholism and unemployment. White traders introduced the Blackfeet to alcohol during the 1700s: the Blackfeet Nation has made preventing and treating alcoholism one of its main goals in recent years. One important weapon in the battle to end alcoholism is The Blackfeet Health and Safety Corps. One of this group's many public services is to teach alcohol awareness to children in reservation schools. The Blackfeet Health and Safety Corps is part of President Bill Clinton's AmeriCorp program, a national plan that enables young people to serve their communities while earning money for college. The Blackfeet Health and Safety Corps is one of two all-Indian AmeriCorp groups in the United States.

Because of the high rate of unemployment plaguing the Montana Blackfeet reservation, programs like the Blackfeet Health and Safety Corps are a welcome opportunity for young people to earn money for further education. Other employers on the reservation are also trying to improve the Blackfeet economy. One of these is the Blackfeet Indian Writing Company, founded in 1972 by current Blackfeet Chief Earl Old Person. The Blackfeet Writing Company manufactures over 15 kinds of pens, pencils, and markers in 29 colors. It churns out over 350,000 writing instruments per day, thanks to over 100 Blackfeet employees. Located just outside the town of Browning, Montana, the Blackfeet Writing Company is the centerpiece of the Blackfeet Industrial Park.

The Blackfeet National Bank of Browning, Montana, is another source of help for the reservation's economy. This bank serves over 7,000 Blackfeet Indians on their remote 1.5 million acre reservation—an area over 58 miles wide.

Necessity spurred the Blackfeet to open their own bank. When the only bank in Browning closed in 1983, the future of Indian businesses was in danger. The tribe took matters into its own hands, investing almost one million dollars to found the Blackfeet National Bank in 1987. The bank is worth over $13 million today.

Tourism is yet another growing field on the Montana Blackfeet reservation. Guests can tour historic sites on the reservation by bus with Blackfeet guides. They can also camp in a historically accurate reproduction of a Blackfeet tepee camp. Campers enjoy listening to traditional storytellers and watching tribal dances during their visits.

In Canada, the Blackfeet are also trying to create job opportunities. There are three Blackfeet reserves in Canada. Canadian Blackfeet share the difficulties faced by Montana Blackfeet in finding work—so they often start their own businesses. The Kainah reserve in Alberta boasts a tribally-managed shopping center and a newspaper. Its residents have also succeeded at building and selling ready-made homes. The North Peigan of Canada manufacture garments.

Despite their efforts, the Blackfeet must still cope with crushing poverty. One recent estimate places the *per capita* income of the Montana Blackfeet at $3,000 per year, and the average *life expectancy* at just 55 years. Indians of other tribes and whites make up roughly 18 percent of the population on the Montana Blackfeet reservation. Although they live peacefully within, the world outside the reservation can still be racially hostile.

Things are changing, however. Non-Indians are becoming more curious about—and respectful of—Native American culture. In 1985, the National Museum of Natural History in Washington, D.C., sent Native American groups in the United States a list of all of the Indian remains in its collection. In March of 1986, the Blackfeet Nation asked the museum to study any remains from Montana to find out if they belonged to the tribe. The remains of 16 people were identified as Blackfeet: they included 15 craniums (the top parts of skulls) and the bones of one person's forearm. An investigation showed that the bones were first robbed from a Blackfeet cemetery in 1892 by American collectors. They were kept in the Army Medical Museum until they were sent to the Smithsonian in 1904. In 1988, the National Museum of Natural History finally sent the bones back to the Blackfeet. The gesture was a way of apologizing for years of displaying tribal remains and *artifacts* in American museums without the Indians' permission.

Although such acts help to improve relations between whites and Indians, many Black-

Although ranching is still an important occupation on the Blackfeet reservation, the tribe values education as the gateway to future prosperity. To that end, they founded the Blackfeet Community College, in Browning, Montana. The College's math and science building is shown here.

feet believe that there is much left to be done. In 1995, the South Peigan Blackfeet living on the Montana reservation made an international appeal to stop commercial oil drilling in an area along the Two Medicine River. The Two Medicine (called the Marias by non-Indians) runs through the southern tip of the reservation. The Peigan argued that they were legally entitled to control the land under the terms of an 1895 treaty. They also said that the land held religious importance for them, and they feared oil drilling would further threaten endangered animals in the area, such as the grey wolf. Like many Native American groups, the Peigan Blackfeet are trying to get the United States government to honor tribal land claims.

The question of whether to keep oil interests out of tribal lands is complex. The Blackfeet themselves have made money by leasing their tribal lands for oil drilling. They also need fossil fuels in order to drive their cars and heat their homes—just like most other Americans. In many ways, the Blackfeet have been *assimilated* into the white world. Some are active members of Christian churches. Every Blackfeet Indian has the right to vote, the obligation to pay taxes (except on businesses run on reservation land), and the freedom to live on or off of a reservation.

Blackfeet Indians in the United States and Canada struggle to keep their traditional beliefs alive in a world that has, in the past, cruelly forced them to live as whites. Some old Blackfeet ways have been revived, though. In 1989, the University of Lethbridge in Alberta, Canada, published a Blackfeet dictionary: a Blackfeet grammar book followed in 1991. Now, the tribe's native language can easily be taught to Blackfeet children.

The chances of a Blackfeet child going to college if he or she wishes to have also improved. Although agriculture and ranching are still the Montana reservation's biggest industries, the Blackfeet wisely recognize that their people will need—as will all Americans—advanced education to land good jobs in the future. This is why the tribe founded Blackfeet Community College in Browning, Montana. The school enables Blackfeet men and women to further their educations without leaving home.

The story of today's Blackfeet Indians is one of balancing old and new ways of life. These lords of the Plains have survived the tragedy of having their domain stolen from them by intruders, and they look forward to the future. Blackfeet people now choose whether to practice Christianity, follow their traditional religion, or blend the best parts of both faiths. Every year in Browning, Montana, they await the arrival of Indian—and non-Indian—guests from around the world for Indian Days, a four-day festival celebrating Blackfeet dances, games, and music. The Blackfeet invite visitors into their world for a short time each year, hoping to bring all people closer to understanding one another. ▲

GLOSSARY

allotment Separate tracts of land assigned to Native Americans under the General Allotment Act of 1887; intended to end tribal landownership and to encourage farming.

anthropologist Scientist who studies human beings and their various ways of life.

artifact Object made by or characteristic of a society during a particular period in history.

assimilate To absorb into a new society.

breechcloth Warm-weather men's garment resembling an apron and worn around the waist.

calumet A ceremonial pipe of the Blackfeet and many other Native American tribes.

culture The beliefs, behaviors, and teachings that govern a group's way of life.

life expectancy The number of years a person can expect to survive.

medicine bundle A collection of objects believed to give its owner magical power and protection, usually kept in a small leather pouch.

nomadic Traveling from place to place to obtain food and other necessities.

oral tradition The practice of transmitting ideas through the spoken word, rather than through a written language.

parfleche A large, envelope-shaped rawhide bag, usually hung on the side of a saddle.

per capita By or for each person in a group.

pictographs Drawings or paintings that depict historical events, words, or quantities.

rites of passage Ceremonies that mark changes in life, such as reaching adulthood or getting married.

reservation A tract of land retained by Native Americans for their own occupation and use (called a reserve in Canada).

shaman A priest who uses magic to see the unknown, to control events, or to heal the sick.

supernatural Belonging to a world beyond the visible universe; the magical and spiritual.

sweat lodge A small tent made of sticks, in which people undergo ritual purification by warming themselves with fire or steam.

taboo A rule against a certain behavior, which is enforced to protect people from supernatural harm.

tepee A cone-shaped tent, usually made of animal skin.

termination A policy during the 1950s that attempted to end government assistance to Native Americans on reservations.

travois A Plains Indian vehicle made from two wooden poles, which trail behind a dog or a horse.

vision quest A sacred ritual in which a person fasts and prays alone for several days, waiting to see or hear messages from the spirit world.

CHRONOLOGY

1541   Native Americans see horses for the first time as mounted Spanish explorers enter North America.

ca. 1770   Horses now play a large part in Native American life; the Blackfeet have become a powerful mounted military culture.

1804–06   The Lewis and Clark expedition; at one point, Meriwether Lewis and an exploring party survive an attack by eight Blackfeet horse raiders, killing two of them.

1808   American John Colter establishes trade with the Crow and the Flathead—two hated Blackfeet enemies. The Blackfeet retaliate by taking him and his partner, John Potts, hostage.

1851   Treaty of Fort Laramie allows settlers to build military outposts and roads on Blackfeet lands; it was drafted and signed without tribe members present.

1855   Lamed Bull's Treaty promises the Blackfeet a total of $35,000 annually in exchange for half of the tribe's territory.

1860   Running Eagle, a famous female Blackfeet warrior, is killed in a battle against the Flathead tribe.

1870   United States Cavalry troops, led by Colonel E. M. Baker, attack a Peigan encampment, killing about 200 Indians.

1883–84   Over 600 Blackfeet men, women, and children starve to death when the government fails to supply the South Peigan of Montana with rations over the winter.

1898   The United States Congress passes the Curtis Act, which outlaws most traditional Native American practices.

1907   The government passes the Blackfeet Allotment Act, violating an 1895 treaty that protected the tribe from the allotment system.

1919–20   Canadian Indian agents are given control over the Kainah reserve's cattle during World War I; much of the herd dies from neglect.

1924   Native Americans are granted full United States citizenship.

1934   The Indian Reorganization Act (IRA) restores power to tribal governments on reservations.

1935 The South Peigan Blackfeet of Montana draft a tribal constitution and found their own business council.

1960 Canada grants its Indians full citizenship.

1972 The Blackfeet Indian Writing Company is founded by current Blackfeet Chief Earl Old Person.

1987 The Blackfeet National Bank opens in Browning, Montana.

1988 The National Museum of Natural History returns the remains of 16 Blackfeet to the tribe; the Blackfeet bones had been stolen from a tribal cemetery in 1892.

FURTHER READING

Andrews, Elaine. *Indians of the Plains*. New York: Benford Books, Inc., 1992.

Brown, Dee. *Dee Brown's Folktales of the Native American*. Illustrated by Louis Mofsie. New York: Henry Holt and Company, Inc., 1993.

Hungry Wolf, Beverly. *The Ways of My Grandmothers*. New York: Quill, 1982.

Lacy, Theresa Jensen. *The Blackfeet*. New York: Chelsea House Publishers, 1995.

Lancaster, Richard. *Piegan*. Garden City, N.Y.: Doubleday, 1966.

Taylor, Colin F. *The Plains Indians*. Avenel, N.J.: Crescent Books, 1994.

INDEX

INDEX

ABOUT THE AUTHOR

ANN-MARIE HENDRICKSON grew up in Los Angeles, California, and graduated from the University of California at Santa Cruz before moving to New York City, where she works for the New York Public Library. She has edited several independent publications, and her writing has appeared in magazines including *Rock Against Sexism* and *Processed World*. She also volunteers for political organizations such as Neither East Nor West, of which she is a founding member.

PICTURE CREDITS

page
2   Illustration by Gary Tong
6–7   Library of Congress, neg. #62-4190
13   American Museum of Natural History, neg. #253757
14   State Historical Society North Dakota Heritage Center
16–17   Library of Congress, neg. #62-01321
19   Library of Congress, neg. #62-101152
24–25   Smithsonian Institution, neg. #56004
28   Library of Congress
33–40   Color section: The Provincial Museum of Alberta, Canada
43   Library of Congress, neg. #62-38862
44   American Museum of Natural History, neg. #2A20323, photo by Walter McClintock
48   National Museum of American Art, Smithsonian Institution, Washington, D.C./Art Resource, NY
50–51   American Museum of Natural History, neg. #122751
52–53   American Museum of Natural History, neg. #319798, photo by Alex J. Rota
54   New York Public Library
60   Glenbow Archives Calgary, Alberta
62   Glenbow Archives Calgary, Alberta
65   Glenbow Archives Calgary, Alberta
66   Library of Congress
69   Library of Congress
72–73   Glenbow Archives Calgary, Alberta
77   Courtesy Blackfeet Community College, photo by Lola Wippert